Also by Joan Shaddox Isom

Poetry

Fox Grapes

Plays

Free Spirits
Boy Medicine
A Pound of Miracles
The Living Forest
Paint Me a Memory
The Visitor

the moon in five disguises

the moon in five disguises

Joan Shaddox Isom

Joan Shaddox Isom
1981

Photography by Jean Bowman

*f*oxmoor Press

First Edition

ACKNOWLEDGMENTS

Some of these poems first appeared in the following periodicals:

The Indian Historian, Moving Out, Oklahoma Woman

Epigraphs and quotes are from the following sources:

Peter Pan by J.M. Barrie, Charles Scribners' Sons, New York. Copyright © 1928 by J.M. Barrie.

Revelations: Diaries of Women, edited by Mary Jane Moffat and Charlotte Painter, Random House, Inc. New York, 1974. Copyright © by Mary Jane Moffat and Charlotte Painter, 1974.

The White Goddess by Robert Graves. Farrar, Straus and Giroux, New York, 1966. Copyright © 1948 by International Authors N.V.

The last three lines in "Mare's Nest" are from an ancient Irish Triad, also quoted from **The White Goddess.**

"Suncatcher" is based on the Cherokee myth of the Spider-grandmother.

Manufactured in the United States of America

Library of Congress Cataloging in Publication Data
Isom, Joan
The Moon in Five Disguises
I. Title
80-70081
ISBN 0-938604-007 Paperbound

Foxmoor Press
Box 47, Rt. 2
Tahlequah, Ok 74464

For the forty-five women with whom I shared some time and space at Women's Voices, 1980, UCSC, Santa Cruz.

Contents

IV

V

the moon in five disguises

I

The Woman in the Photograph Wears Victory Red Lipstick

The Woman in the Photograph Wears Victory Red Lipstick

Like swimming under water,
the light loses you.
You float in the damp air.
Blue and green goblets
on the window ledge try to collect
the afternoon sun and filter it into the room.

Antimacassars coil around the arms
of overstuffed chairs.
Satin pillows gleam like sunfish
on the window seat.
One reads: "To my Sweetheart,
U.S. Army, 1944."
Two flags cross above its pink and gold poem
that speaks of love and honor.

Darting her hand into the grotto
of the china cabinet, she clutches something,
runs to the window.
"If I could only see to tell!"she cries.
I reach up a forefinger to make a circle
on the coated pane. A bubble of light
holds the woman in the photograph.
"Me," she whispers, "at the USO Club."

I Should Have Run for Watermelon Queen

A whistling girl
and a crowing hen
always come
to some bad end.

Mamma, you always warned me about bouncing
green peaches off boys' heads.
Tried your best to dress me in pink pinafores;
gave up after you saw me come home with the skirts
torn off at the waist from fights with Willis Bradford.

I remember when you called me into the house
one hot night in the 'fifties
as you watched the Miss America Pageant on television.
You sat, slack body bent into accusations
while all the dazzling daughters
came together in their virginal dance
down the walkway.

"See," you said. "Her first break was being chosen
Cucumber queen of Leeds Creek, Louisiana--
you just have to make a start. That's all."

Watching you that night I almost felt pity,
wanted to say, "You win, Mamma,
I'll get me some red ankle-strap shoes,
low-cut dress (anything but pink)
run for Cotton Maid or Watermelon Queen,"
but I didn't say it.

Now, at ninety years of age,
you still have a way of looking at my scrubby jeans,
splayed sandals, big restless hands.
I get the message. I always did.

You don't give up though.
I have to hand it to you,
for now, when I visit, you always
prop up on an inquisitive elbow,
question me as I am leaving,
"Why don't you get yourself a little dress
 and put on some makeup?
Your cake's not baked yet, you know."

Coping

Her therapist, Dr. Rubel (who is considered quite good)
told her "Don't ever let one bad thought in
or it will bring its relatives and stay until
you are as broken as a housewife trying to stretch
her hospitality to include thirty in-laws."

She did allow one in, however, that ninth day of rain,
thinking she would have it stay only for tea,
but when it stuck its foot in her door
and motioned for all its hideous companions to follow
she knew she was lost.
They filed in, all carrying luggage, paper sacks
full of underwear, talcum, toothpaste, paperbacks,
which they plunked down in her bedroom without even
a by-your-leave.
One even opened her last can of onion soup
and ate it with a horrid smacking of its lips.
When she complained, it replied that she should look upon
the incident as a growth experience.

After the Ten O'clock news, they all rose
with the regimentation of a chorus line
and tripped and kicked in perfect time
back to her bedroom, telling her all the while
how fortunate she was to have booked
the "Complete Package."

They unpacked, packed, unpacked
strange unrelated objects, glass fishing floats,
a master's thesis on Rilke, a worn burgundy colored
house slipper, shaped to some foot
that seemed vaguely familiar to her,
travel brochures of the south of France,
(how they smirked as if they knew something she didn't.)

In the end, she joined them, of course,
taking down her not-too-new, not-too-old luggage
and after some thought, packing her
"Girl of the Year" trophy,
a crèche missing an angel and a baby,
a picture of herself in her prom dress,
and a list of things to do when the weather warmed.
After some nudging, they moved over
and let her join them in their choreographed dance
billed as "A Sensible, Well-adjusted Existence"
and no one noticed her absence until
she missed her appointment with Dr. Rubel on Thursday.
When the good doctor became concerned
and called at her home,
he found her calm and rational, the perfect hostess.
She told him she needed no more sessions
and was coping quite well.
Bidding him goodbye, she hurried down the hall, saying
that she was very busy with new projects,
which prompted Dr. Rubel to remark to his receptionist
later that afternoon, how beautifully Mrs. Brownell
had adjusted to middle age.

...We need only discover within ourselves how and when to call upon either of the functions we need--a task that may, like the via longissima of the alchemists, take more lives than one...

Charlotte Painter

Geminate

You need her, the woman with cathedrals blazing
in her eyes, symphonies pouring from her gut.
She shines white-hot. That burning is both
a cleansing and a forging.
Surely you felt a tearing when she split away
at your conception. She has dined at the tables
of your more visionary brothers. You see their names.
Children mumble their birth and death dates.

Little-shadow-of-yourself; it could be a twinning.
She can fit her body to yours, soft
where you are sinewy, flowing into your shallow places.
It is not the Muse you need in the hours before dawn
when the pages of the second draft crawl about your feet.

No witch; she can cross water. Like the Twins,
you two can easily barter back and forth
in that boat between camps.
Banquets served at other tables have sufficed
until this time,
but now I think she is coming for you.
Make ready; travel light.
She is a tracker under a different set of stars.
Mark this.

Old Woman on a Stick

Helpless, I hang here,
dress-tail full of wind.
Breezes flap my faded skirts;
mice nest in my pockets.
Curse the one who created me,
left me out here to guard his fields
(at least that's what he said)
but this land has grown only cockleburrs
and nettles for a decade.

He used to visit me often,
told me I was a crazed old harpy
who lived just to nag his life away.
Strange he should say that to one
who can't talk back, for when he painted my face
he left a blank space where my mouth should have been.

One day he brought me a fine bonnet,
tied it on me, laughing like a loon all the while.
"Take the old hag's hat! She won't need it again!"
I never saw him after that.

He could have had the decency to take me down,
stow me in the barnloft where the owls and swallows
would keep me company,
but he has abandoned me here to flap and turn,
aimless as an old one fumbling for firewood in the dark.

My brains are leaking out around my ears;
the birds keep stealing my stuffing for nests.
To be impaled here on a stick
by a good-for-naught wretch!

But if this winter's wind
is as strong as last,
I just might take flight from this pole
and visit him some dark of the moon.

What would he say if he found the old hag
back in his bed?

Nursing Home Patient; Room 102

Look, Mother, a new room-mate.
What is your name?
  My name? Thurston Burnett, that was my husband's name.
  We gave credit to everyone at our store
  and that's why we went broke.

But your name, I persisted,
what is your name?
  Burnett! (as if I were simple) Thurston Burnett!

Later, over her bed, I read it:
Oma Burnett; Dr. Colton, regular diet.

Hello, Oma.
She looked at me as if she didn't know who Oma was.

Camouflage

Dust on the windowpane
spreads a comforting film

ball of lint on the table
mars the lacquered surface

four o'clock sun filters
sepia light that holds me
against water-marked wallpaper

I leave no shadow.

Slick-picker

Old stealer of feel goods,
stays on her steps all night
(her door is unlocked.)
She hears him laughing,
knows he is holding up wildcat whiskey
in a Mason jar, only a corner
between him and the moon.

At dawn he gets up
rides off whistling
back to something or someone
(he could do better)

She whispers:
I am lean; I am brown
I taste of tequila and salt.

Aw, girl! Let him go!
He wouldn't know a good thing
if he ran smack into it!

II

The Moon in Five Disguises

The Moon in Five Disguises

It's your pock-marked face again
pressing through the lattice.
You are losing your touch, you know
for this final disguise fools no one
even as you rattle the bones
of your cumbersome cart
past my tipsy gate-post.

I believed in you once; why not?
You had all the trappings:
wind harp, moon flowers, silver shoon.
"Do you know where the mermaids play?"
"Second to the right and straight on
'till morning" you called, crooking a finger
as you rushed by me.

I followed your form, a bright balloon.
You lifted me over gentle jungles
alive with soft-eyed tigers and cinnamon trees.
The plunge was swift and fierce.

After that we made a sort of truce.
I even planted by your lantern, tilled the soil,
readied myself for harvest,
but one night you broke into a thousand howling pieces,
went scrabbling away, leaving me mute
among my blighted crops.

Now, watching from my window,
I know with a sudden certainty
this is no masquerade
and as the hollow clop of your nag's hooves
echoes in the streets, I turn
to tie them up in flattened bundles.
Paper-thin little bodies,
you toss on your cart
with barely a glance and drive away.

What will you do with them?
Where will you take them?

"Shush, child"
an old woman beckons me back up the stairs
and I hear you crying up to other windows

New lamps for old!
New lamps for old!

Homunculus

I must be truthful,
you are on a fool's errand, pretty boy,
if you expect to find a place
under my ribs (I have made my choice.)
This womb is starting to atrophy.
You ought to materialize before robust women
who could birth you and never give a second thought,
but you keep appearing to me at odd hours, singing,
wanting to play. Child of mind, what this time?
A game of "Feed the Crow"?
You laugh as I catch your finger
in my handtrap. You laugh and the sound
draws me down to childhood.
We make mudcakes, pressing in pebble raisins, stamping
them with palm prints. Mine grow larger as I grow older,
but you remain ever young.
Ah, baby, what's the good of it?
But you are so quick and fine
I succumb and sing a nonsense rhyme
to the quiet uncluttered room:

Littleboynevergrow
Cat's cradle, feed the crow
Could have others; just wants me
Littleboyneverbe.

Antidote

I guess we must have fancied ourselves
some kind of Moon Children,
muttering magic at midnight,
sticking pins in a wax doll.
You said it looked exactly like Miss Doaks,
our ninth grade math teacher, as you gleefully pierced
its heart with a pin.

We were careful, of course, to keep behind
locked doors, having been warned we were consorting
with evil.
You must have been half afraid the charms
just might work, for I saw you clutching
the gold cross at your throat.

Inseparable, that's what they said of us,
but one day we sat over our tea
with nothing to talk about.

Last week you called, asking me to visit,
saying a mutual friend had given you my number.
I arrived, noting your apothecary jar
now held quick-mix recipes.
I couldn't find a wink of quicksilver in the house.
Your totems whirred and blended on the counter-top
while mine, yellow pads filled with notes
legible only to me, I left tucked under my pillow.

It didn't matter, I told myself, for each of us
had mixed herself a proper antidote.

Touch-me-not

How effortless to await a miracle
when she was certain none would occur,
but it burst upon her in middle age
and she reacted as a child
who, upon surviving a tonsilectomy,
blinks, bedazzled, seeking affirmation
from faces floating above.
How long, she wonders, can vital signs
apex this sweet delirium
without total collapse?
Racked by feverdream fantasies
she scopes a squint-eyed moonscape
whimpers
for some older, calmer existence.

Relief comes in summer;
the miracle, now, that she can suture up
thick-edged similarity of days
sliding into days sliding into days.
Grateful, she scalpels them into identical strips
to be packaged and labeled:
noli me tangere

Earth-anchored

This season, of all seasons
my body is cumbersome

as a fat bear ready for hibernation
the slim arrow of my shadow

against the dry grass denies this
but I am not appeased

in a time when everything is taking flight
blackbirds, milk-weed fluff, dying leaves

I stand ponderous, earth-anchored
raising my face to the cold drizzle

I search for southbound geese
invisible behind low clouds

this body, still awkward on two legs, wants
to belong to the wind, but my wings

have atrophied away to a small piece
of triangular skin between my arms and shoulders

reminding me how close I came
to escaping the anchor that holds me.

Dog Days

Sirius, the Dog Star, paces the sun by day;
tonight the earth's mouth is open
sending a searing breath
to hone the insects' song
to a cutting edge of pure pain.

A pick-up truck rattles to a halt
in the dust-choked lane.
A woman in a pale dress gets out.
She is alone. Her voice is the scream
of a trapped animal.
Everything she has ever wanted to say
rolls out and out. She must speak it all.
When she has finished she gets back
into the truck and drives away.

Something ugly and crazed has this hour
by the nape of the neck and won't let go.
Somewhere a child whimpers and begs
for the night to end.

Companions

When Old Age raps on my window and beckons
with bony finger, I'll not follow her
behind closed shutters to measure out my life
with nose drops at 2:00 pm, a teaspoon of tonic
before Lawrence Welk. No...

I will tell her to come with me
and I will take her on the handlebars of my bicycle
and whizz her through the streets,
both of us in blue jeans, our hair quite gray,
and they will say,
"Look at those two old ladies!
They don't know how to grow old with dignity!"

So, maybe we'll stop by for Dignity,
pull her protesting, to the park,
strip off her rolled-down hose,
show her how to run barefoot, fly kites,
pet mangy dogs
and rouge her mouth with red popsicles.

We'll tie a bright balloon to the handlebars
as we ride home at dusk, singing a bawdy song,
and Dignity, still drunk from the Ferris-wheel,
her hat askew, will wave a wistful goodbye
as we careen around the corner, Old Age and I,
giving one last exuberant cry.

Arrangements

Washing the peas
I drop one into the bowl.
It rolls about, re-adjusts itself,
settles into patterns with the others.

We stand by empty doors, waiting
for a word, a question.

Are you going to market?
Have you fed the cats?
Are you wearing that hat?
Are you going to wed?

I drop the peas into boiling water.
They scarcely bubble and squeak
before they settle into soup.

III

Waiting out the Cold

Waiting out the Cold

It takes a frost to ripen this fruit.
The little orbs hang in the sun and wait
for the cold, unmindful of the myth
they carry in their seeds.

A boy once told me:

> "Eat a persimmon; break open a seed,
> find there a knife, fork or spoon
> within the seed's heart."

The tree goes about its task
budding, bearing, releasing fruit
season after season, ignoring prophecies.

We seed in any sign and drop our fruit.
Like the tree, we have myths others have hung
upon us. Long into the nights we pore
over words that others have written,
only a few daring to bear the cold of closed rooms,
daring to add our own line.

Chicken Money

Mamma always liked to read.
When the magazine salesman
drove up the lane and stopped
to give her his pitch,
she stood there over the wash tub
listening to all the slick, multi-color dreams
he told so well.
One-hundred and thirty-seven pages
guaranteed to transport a person
clear out of the heat and dirt of Adair County.

Finally, when he finished, she smoothed
back her hair, dried her hands on her apron and said,
"You kids go and run down one of those old hens
to pay this man for a subscription to his magazine.
You'll take a chicken, won't you"?
He did. It was the depression and a fat hen
was as good as money in his pocket.

People Wouldn't Sleep at all if They Could Help It

People fear sleep.
At the breakfast table they recite
their litany of thanksgivings
for having survived another night.

"'I woke up and couldn't go back to sleep,
the moon was bright as day."
"I thought I heard the 'phone ring
but there was no one on the line
when I answered it."
"I heard a cat fight, but it was too cold
to get up and see about it."

The mother places hot food on the table.
The grandmother cups her hands around
the warm coffee mug.
Children hit and pinch each other
(it is good to feel firm flesh after dreams.)

In the diner, the truckers watch
the pink-skirted waitress as she moves
between the counters.

Seasonal Wisdom

Last night the first frost fell.
Today, everything is letting go.
The leaves fall, no scar marking the tree
where they have been.
Persimmons thump softly
against frozen ground.
Thistle-down drifts against
the earth's curve,
finally settles into a heap
of dry leaves.
The cat, already casting summer
behind her, curls herself
into a tight ball on the step.
A woman at a window stands staring;
her gaze cannot get past the sill.
Hands flutter up, turning
into fists jammed into dry eye-sockets.
She ponders the age-old seasonal wisdom
of letting go
and wonders why she cannot.

GYPSY MOTHS SWARM !
Newspaper headline proclaims
The article reads:
Too many people are taking gypsy moths
along with them when they move to a new area,
according to U.S. Department of Agriculture
officials. Cagey gypsy moths creep
into vans and campers, lay their eggs
and send them on the road.
Not content to thrive in one spot
these designing females are sending
their children to colonize states everywhere.

The government is trying to trap these gypsies
in cardboard devices baited
with synthetic sex lures.

The government says trapping one or two moths
does not always mean a new infestation
but officials are monitoring her larvae closely.
"She bears watching' one official says.

Uninvited Guest

Some kind of truce
I should have made with you
a long time ago.
We could have learned to tolerate each other
but I kept flinging you out
like the bony old cat
someone dropped off at my gate.
I knew better than to feed you.
My grandmother told me that.
She said "Child, don't ever start it
or you will have to keep it up."

Oh, I knew you were still out there
skulking under the forsythia bush

biding your time,
but I thought I could drown out your whine
with the music box. I wound it up tightly,
danced around the room, even tried to banish
your odor with bayberry candles, donned
a scarlet caftan, stacked gaudy magazines
on every table.
But on one bright cover, I read your name, evidence
that you had plagued others before me,
and opening the pages, I read a list of useless things
I had tried already; "Ten Ways to Dispel Loneliness."

IV

Rituals

Rituals

People still bring food
in times of sickness and death,
busy themselves in the kitchen
heating up soup,
cutting cakes, making coffee,
going through these rituals,
making sure everyone eats.
We chew dutifully, trying to swallow,
trying to comfort them.

Planting by the Signs

I

If you strain for it, it won't happen
like a name you're trying too hard to remember.
Granny Henshaw always announced in a loud voice
"I'm looking for my thimble!"
when she was really looking for her glasses.
The heart is a strange organ.
Like Granny, it shouts
"I'm really looking for my scarab ring,
my green and gold quilt, my sea shell,
my rock from the Oregon coast."
Remember when we complained that all
the driftwood was picked over? Picked over
like the dolls on Christmas Eve
when they're missing one shoe and would cry
about it if their eyes weren't pushed
back into their heads, when picture frames
with corners pulled apart are two for one
and Clark Gable leers, not knowing he's going
at a reduced rate on the bargain table.

II

Queen of Hearts, you meddling old crone
have blown dust across empty rooms
into a thousand eyes. Like the whirlwind on the parking lot,
you go on forever.
"That trash must be thousands of feet high" he said.
We stayed to watch the wind scoop up everything that day.
After all, it was March, the season for living.

III

We never did get it right
this planting by the signs.
Was it the Twins for cucumbers and melons
and Taurus for root crops?
And then there was the dark and light
of the moon to consider.
Almanacs don't give clear instructions
these days, and just as before,
pastures get greener from all the bone marrow;
we plant seeds and forget what sign we planted in.

Crèche

Cleaning out the junk room,
I came across the battered crèche
left on the shelf for the last two seasons.
Only one smug camel smiled his presence
at the birthing this year.
He survived, no doubt, because he was lying down
feet tucked up under him, his brothers
long ago lost their legs and were tossed out
in after-Christmas trash.

Joseph was missing his staff;
Mary had her face to the wall
surrounded by a donkey, a kind cow,
three wise men who looked ordinary if not slow,
and a bewildered lamb wondering where
the shepherd boy had gone.

And you, little plaster baby,
lying with arms outstretched, don't think
I blame you for any of it.
True, we aren't communicating these days
but I hope you understand
I am seized with a kind of numbness
that excludes anything else. I must concentrate
to get through these rituals intact.

Don't think I won't take you out of the closet
although I can't say exactly when.
You and I, baby, are not in a cold war, exactly
but I can't turn your mother around to croon over you
for at least another year.

Be patient; that's what you told me
concerning grief's overdue departure
and don't throw your pink little arms out in astonishment
at the petulance you knew I was capable of
all along.

Egg Day

(Overheard in the women's room of a cafeteria)

I can't go tomorrow. It's egg day.

What?

Egg day. You know.

Egg Day?

Yes. I buy my eggs from this man who delivers them from his farm.

I thought you bought your eggs at Safeway.

Safeway! Ha! Even the ones they mark "extra large" are not as nice as the ones I get from the Egg Man, and his are almost all double-yolked!

Well, I'd planned for you to go with me. You can always get your eggs at the market.

Oh, no. I can't go tomorrow. I never plan anything on egg day.

Witching for Water

Do you witch wells for the drillers?

Oh, no, I don't do it for the well drillers,
just friends and neighbors, this one and that.

How did you learn to locate water?

No learning to it. I just went out,
cut a peach tree limb, forked, like this,
and started witching one time when I was young.

Don't you have to hold the stick a certain way?

Oh, yes, someone showed me--I forget just who.
You walk and walk and when you cross water
the stick turns in your hand, twists, sort of.
You tell them there is water here, and there is,
every time.

Can anyone do it?

No, not everyone.

Why can you do it? Is it magic?

Magic? I never thought about it.
Maybe. I just do it. I don't think.
It works though. I can witch from north to south,
find water, then witch from east to west, criss-cross,
and the stick will turn at the same place every time.

I don't think. I just do it.

V

Woman of the Owl Clan

Woman of the Owl Clan

You talked off and on all summer in the woods
west of my house, your voice a higher pitch
than your mate's deeper cry. Once I saw
your shadow in the trees, heard the birds
screech a warning. Now, on the first night
of the Ice-forming-moon, your call is insistent,
demanding. You want me.
I rise from a warm bed, softly, carefully
removing his arm that lies across me,
creep to the door and open it. The frost
bites at my bare skin. Again, you call
and I feel my finger bones becoming feather spine.
My body grows lighter; toes and fingers
become talons, eyes in the dark are heavy moons.
I can twist my head three-quarters of a turn
to spot a rodent a hundred feet beneath me
in a fence row. You call again.

I mount the night sky, wings slicing open
the cold, cutting a path to Sparrow-hawk Mountain.
You find me there; together we go about
this night business, talking to the vixen
who turns translucent eyes up from dark ridges.
You teach me to distinguish shadow from form,
wind song from night voices; how to float
and stall, dropping like a stone upon our prey.
I tremble between pity and power as we rip
the bodies of the furry ones, stripping
the bones until they shine clean. Carelessly,
you flick aside our leavings, reminding me
"Compassion is not the way of our clan."

Then, seeing the light in the east,
you wheel after a moon that has gone
to follow the dark, and I watch the night
take you both back into itself, night
that knows the difference between Owl and Woman.

I drop, and as I fall, my bird bones thicken,
fingers blunt, fit only for opening doors. I enter the house
to creep down beside him. He sighs in his sleep,
moves to adjust his body to fit the body
that is once more woman-form. I lie awake, listening,
until
in the woods west of my house, you call,
telling me you are my Sister-Who-Waits.

Sun-catcher (from a Cherokee myth)

Crouched in darkness
we are!
Who will catch the sun
and bring it to us?
the people cried.

Buzzard danced before them.
I will catch the sun!
Not just a little piece,
but the whole big ball!
he croaked as he flew higher, higher.

Owl laughed
and muttered about those
who fly too high
before he blinked himself
back to sleep.

Poor old Buzzard came back with his head
singed bald, and no sun.

I will catch the sun!
Old Possum preened himself,
and flaunting his fluffy tail
he went off, climbing, climbing
clear up to the sun.
Owl woke again, too amazed to hoot,
went back to sleep.

Poor old Possum came back
all squinty-eyed
dragging his tail burned bare
by the sun he had left behind.

Crouched in darkness
forever we will be!
the People wailed.

Then a crackly-thin little whisper
from the dry grass
I will catch the sun!

Who's that? Owl hooted.
Spider-grandmother?
The People laughed.
Spider-grandmother!
What a spinner of dreams!

She did not argue
but took her little clay bowl
still damp from the molding
and spun a web as she went
clear up to the sun.

For days she spun and climbed,
climbed and spun.
In the darkness below
they forgot about her
and went to sleep.

Raven saw it first,
a glow in the east.
He squawked to the others,
It's the sun!
At least a piece of it,
in Spider-grandmother's little clay bowl!

I knew she could do it all the time,
Owl remarked as he flew away to the woods
where the dark had gone to hide.

I have caught the sun for you
Spider-grandmother said.
Now leave me alone
for I have clay pots to make
and the sun will bake them
with his fire.

And you, she told the People,
can find your own use for the sun!

The Marks on the Trees are for You

She told me to stay here, hidden,
whispering of the dangers in the forest
and how she needed to run swiftly.
Stripping herself of all totems,
she stood naked, bending over me,
carefully breaking branches, building
a hiding-place, a nest, a grave?
(I remembered how elephants cover
their dead with branches.)

It was then I knew she was not coming back.
I did not weep nor beg,
but watched her walk away.
Her body held itself differently;
her eyes were fixed on a far point.

Where the trees began, she turned,
shouted back at me,
"If I don't return, you can follow.
The marks on the trees are for you.
It has to be this way."
She mouthed the words to the wind
for I was no longer listening.

Now, years later, rumors from across the river
tell of a strange old hag
who still searches among the sleepers at night,
muttering about something she once possessed
and can't remember where she left it.

Mare's Nest

She has been snarling herself in the hair
of your dreams since you saw first-light;
be sure, she will come for you some night
when you no longer watch the empty road
in the rain. Listen to one who has ridden
her more than once. It will be like this...

Arching her long neck over your sill,
she tugs the covers from your sleeping form.
The crescent moon about her death-white neck
gleams a warning, but you rise and go to her,
throwing a leg over her back. You knot
your hands in the coarseness of her mane
and find you cannot loosen your grasp.
Her pale fillies float behind you like
nine winter moons.
She is so swift no thoroughbred can pace her.
Some try and are found dead in their stables
at dawn.

If you bend your head and whisper to her these words:
  "O Rhiannon, my Great Queen"
she will show you her nests caught
like clouds in the yew tree roots. Lined
with her white hair, they hold no new foal,
only bones. Before she takes you back to your bed
she will ask a question, and you must
answer thusly, or your bones will litter her nest:

"O Rhiannon, it is death
to mock, to love or to be
a poet."

Muse-birth

Water had been long before Fire, and lonely.
Lightening, perhaps pitying him,
set her blazing one night in the top
of a dead tree
and her brilliance brought him blinking
from his sleep among dark rushes.

Once he had seen her flash and felt her heat
he knew he must possess her
but he was patient, swirling slyly over smooth stones
in his bed, pretending to busy himself
propelling Water-walker or beguiling Bottom Creeper
to the top
all the while, watching.

He wanted to pour himself over her.
He sang of it as he fell through space
to bottomless pools where he lay languid
with Spoon-bill and murmured his plan
to the cool mud.
She knew; she was watching him also, until
one day, mesmerized by a sun-dog,
dreaming perhaps, of older beginnings,
she was caught off-guard.
There was a hissing and a small silence
when they saw what their passion had produced.
He took flight back to his bed
and she went feeding wildly away
through the rushes along his banks.

But it could not last, this separateness,
being opposites, they could not stay apart,
yet knowing what she knows, she chose to live
in the flash of Owl's eye
and he secluded himself in the steam of Owl's breath,
together, yet apart.

They did not speak of the Woman-child they held in awe,
clothed in a pure white vapor, visible only
to a certain few who shall be known as
Those-who-are-called-tellers-of-dreams.

"My heart is five lotuses. You building these five into one, dance and swell in my mind."